BIGSBY TIMBER CO.

GW00393801

A Gift For:

From:

Mushroom Ridge

8300

Ruby Creek

9200

Mount Pahrump

7100

The Gazette

Mystery in woods?

A local man claims to have seen large furry creature roaming the heavily wooded areas around the old Bigsby Timber Company site. "He's a big ...," said a Mr. Jasper of

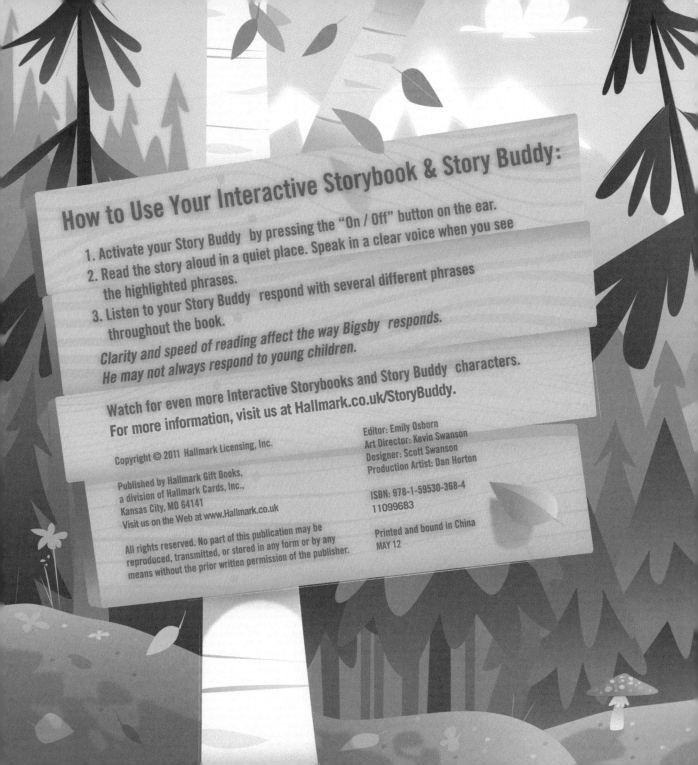

How to Use Your Interactive Storybook & Story Buddy:

1. Activate your Story Buddy by pressing the "On / Off" button on the ear.
2. Read the story aloud in a quiet place. Speak in a clear voice when you see the highlighted phrases.
3. Listen to your Story Buddy respond with several different phrases throughout the book.

Clarity and speed of reading affect the way Bigsby responds.

He may not always respond to young children.

Watch for even more Interactive Storybooks and Story Buddy characters.

For more information, visit us at Hallmark.co.uk/StoryBuddy.

Copyright © 2011 Hallmark Licensing, Inc.

Published by Hallmark Gift Books,
a division of Hallmark Cards, Inc.,
Kansas City, MO 64141
Visit us on the Web at www.Hallmark.co.uk

Editor: Emily Osborn
Art Director: Kevin Swanson
Designer: Scott Swanson
Production Artist: Dan Horton

ISBN: 978-1-59530-368-4
11099683

Printed and bound in China
MAY 12

BOOK 1

BIGSBY's
Best Friend

Hallmark

Written by Jake Gahr . Illustrated by Bob Kolar
Character & Concept by Scott Swanson

In a great green forest lived a huge furry
creature named Bigsby. Bigsby didn't have many
friends because he was an extremely shy guy.

One day a boy named Sam moved into a house near the forest. Moving was boring and Sam had nothing to do. So when he noticed a large footprint on the ground, he followed it.

Footprints always lead to feet...and legs...and that's just what Sam bumped into that day. The huge feet and legs of Bigsby. Bigsby smiled nervously, and waved.

"Holy hair balls!" Sam exclaimed. "Hello. I'm Sam. I'm new in town. What's your name?" But Bigsby said nothing, because he was an extremely shy guy.

Sam smiled. "You know, you're pretty shy for such a big thing."

When he heard "BIG," Bigsby thought Sam was trying to say his name. So he excitedly nodded his big shaggy head and said, "Uh-huh. Bigsby."

Sam laughed. "Ha ha. No, I said you're BIG." Bigsby
pointed to the name on his shoe. "BIGS-BY." Sam said,
"Ooh! I get it! Well then, it's nice to meet you!"

Then, out of nowhere, Sam touched Bigsby's knee. "Tag! You're it!" Bigsby was confused.

Sam tagged him again. "Come on. Let's play!" He ran away. Then Bigsby understood and went to chase after him. Suddenly they heard someone coming. A man and his dog were walking towards them. Bigsby needed to hide, and fast, because he was an extremely shy guy.

Sam realised that his new friend was bashful. Quickly he helped Bigsby hide. The man walked up to Sam. "Hello, I'm Mr. Jasper."

"Hi. I'm Sam." But Sam knew Mr. Jasper was his new neighbour.

"You'd better watch out," Mr. Jasper said. "There's a furry creature on the loose...about the size of this tree here." Mr. Jasper leaned against the "tree." "I've been looking for this guy for years...so if you ever see him, let me know. Okay?"

Sam nodded.

"Wow, that was close," Sam said. "I wonder why Mr. Jasper wants to find you so badly." Bigsby shook his head and shrugged.

Sam visited Bigsby every day after that. Bigsby
showed Sam how to juggle. They played tag, jumped
in piles of leaves, and told jokes.

"Why don't sharks eat clowns?" Sam said. "Because they taste funny!" Bigsby thought it was very funny.

In the winter, they went sledging and built igloos. They had snowball fights and played swords with icicles. Sam made peanut butter and sardine sandwiches, Bigsby's favourite. But one day, their fun almost came to an end.

The two friends were in the forest having
a snowball fight when they saw Mr. Jasper
walking around. Bigsby grabbed some
branches to disguise himself as a tree.
Since the branches didn't have leaves this
time, they weren't a very good disguise. "I
think I saw him over here," said Mr. Jasper.
Bigsby felt a shiver up his back.

Sam had a great idea and told Bigsby to roll around in the snow. Bigsby stood up just in time. "Hello again, Mr. Jasper."

"Say, Sam, have you seen that large furry creature around here?" Mr. Jasper asked. Sam shook his head. Mr. Jasper stared at the snowman. "He's about the same size as your snowman there."

As Mr. Jasper walked away, Sam and his "snowman" laughed. Bigsby thought it was very funny.

Sam climbed onto Bigsby's shoulders.
"Don't worry, Bigsby. I'll never let him find you,"
said Sam. He pointed to their shadow. "You
know what? We don't have to worry about
anything or anyone, because together, we're
the biggest, best thing in the whole forest!"
Bigsby nodded.

Soon it was time to say good night. Sam couldn't wait until their next big adventure. He wrapped his arms around Bigsby's furry neck and said, "Bigsby, you're the best friend a kid could ever have."

Did you have fun reading with Bigsby? We would lov to hear from you!

Please send your comments to:
Hallmark Book Feedback
Bingley Road
Bradford
West Yorkshire, BD9 6SD

Or e-mail us at:
gifts@hallmark-uk.com

BIGSBY TIMBER CO.
"We cut 'em all the way down!"

S	M	T	W	T	F	S
		1	2	3	4	5
6	7	8	9	10	11	12
13	14	15	16	17	18	19
20	21	22	23	24	25	26
27	28	29	30			

Found a footprint on the mushroom ridge trail

seen him by Ruby creek!

Gimlin ass
8300
Bluff Creek
Lake Patterson